I Want a

Written by Judith Nicholls
Illustrated by Debbie Clark

Collins *Educational*
An imprint of HarperCollins*Publishers*

"No!" said Mum."No party this time. Unless...
you want to plan it?"
"That's easy," grinned Pete. "What do I have to do?"
"You tell me," smiled Mum.
Pete started to make a list.

"There!" said Pete. "Finished!"

"Is that it?" asked Mum, and she laughed so much she nearly cried.
"When is this party?" she asked. "And are we going to make the sandwiches *before* we ask your friends to come?"

She took down the calendar and Pete filled in some of the spaces.

JUNE

Mon 15		**Mon 22**	Buy balloons!
Tues 16		**Tues 23**	
Wed 17		**Wed 24**	
Thurs 18		**Thurs 25**	Buy food
Fri 19		**Fri 26**	Make flapjacks. Order more milk.
Sat 20	Send invitations	**Sat 27**	PETE'S PARTY!
Sun 21		**Sun 28**	

“There!” said Pete. “Now I’ve finished!’

"You'll have to invite Granny," said Mum.
Pete fetched his pencil.

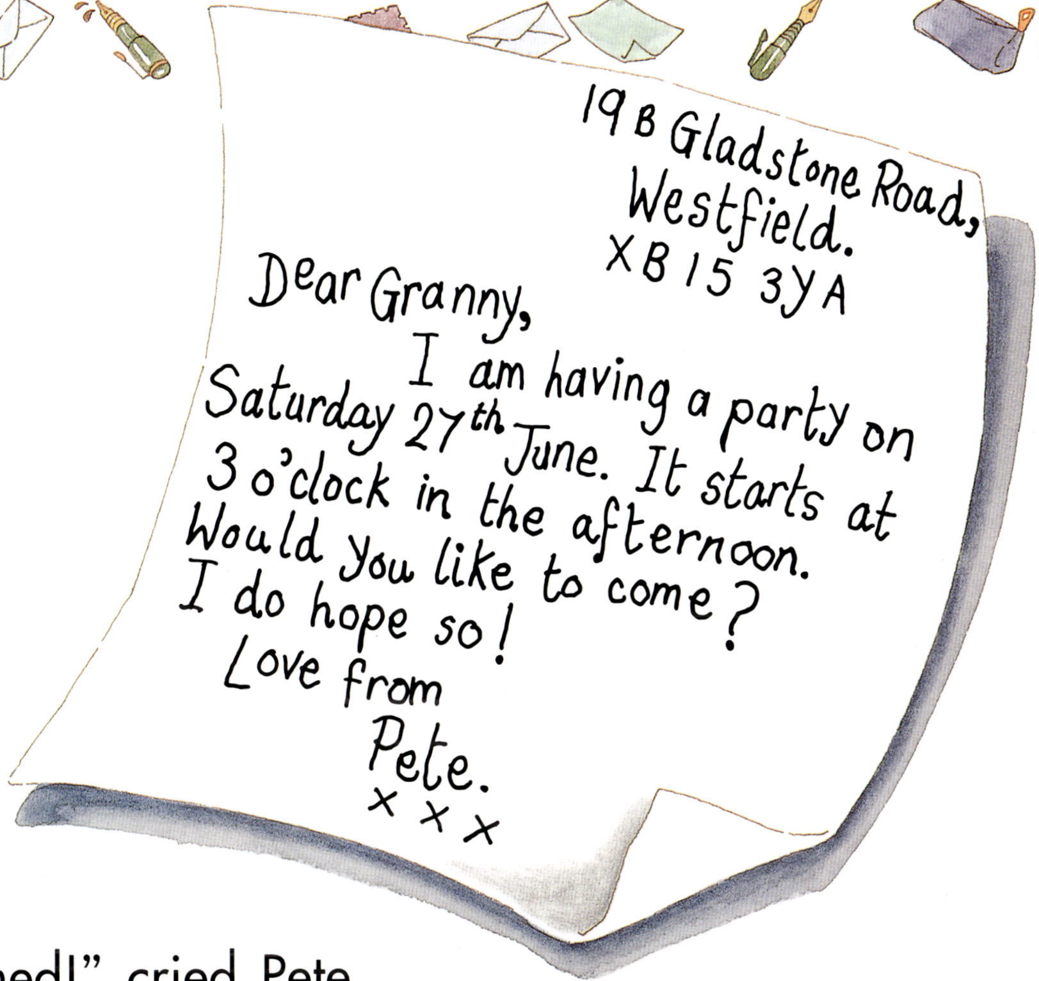

19 B Gladstone Road,
Westfield.
XB15 3YA

Dear Granny,

I am having a party on Saturday 27th June. It starts at 3 o'clock in the afternoon. Would you like to come? I do hope so!

Love from

Pete.

x x x

"Finished!" cried Pete.

“What about all your friends?” demanded Mum.
“Whoops! I nearly forgot!” laughed Pete.
Mum gave him some invitation cards from her drawer and Pete started to fill them in.

"All finished!" yelled Pete.

"What are we going to eat at your party?"
Mum wanted to know.
Pete knew that.

"That's it!" yelled Pete. "I've finished!"

“I haven’t got all those things in my cupboard,” Mum groaned.
Pete sighed and took out his pencil again.

"There!" cried Pete. "I've worked it out!"

“We can order the milk from our milkman,”
Mum reminded him.
Pete wrote a note for the milkman ready for
the day before the party.

“Now I’ve *really* finished!” cried Pete.

“Do you know how to make flapjacks?” asked Mum. Pete took down the big cookbook and looked in the index for *flapjacks*.

"Found it!" yelled Pete. "It's on page 25!"

“Do they take long to make?” Mum wondered.
“I’ll find out,” answered Pete.

Flapjacks

Ingredients

150g butter
75g brown sugar
75g treacle or honey
225g porridge oats

Method

1. Put the butter, sugar and treacle or honey in a pan. Melt slowly over a gentle heat. Do not boil. Remove from heat.
2. Mix the oats in well.
3. Press mixture into greased tin.
4. Bake in centre of oven at 180° Celsius (Gas mark 4) for about 25 minutes or until golden brown.
5. Divide into 12 portions while still warm and leave to cool.

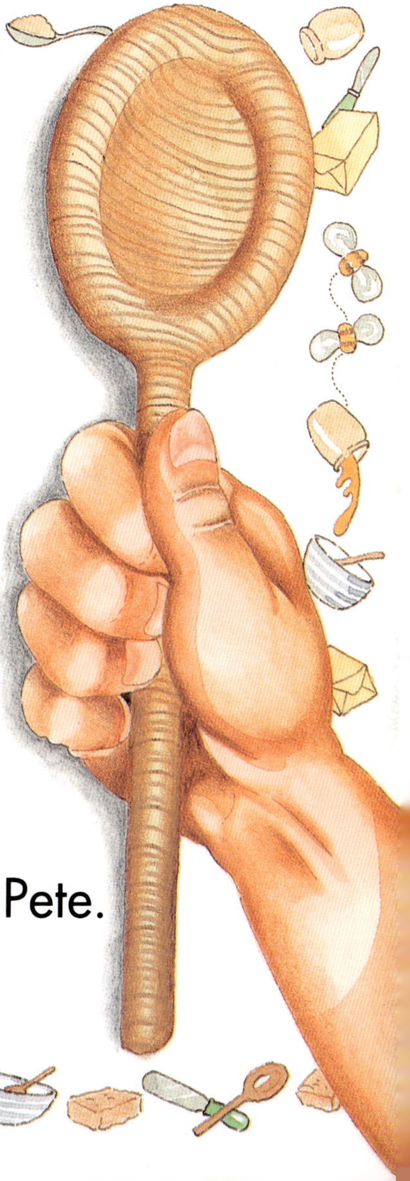

“They don’t take long at all,” announced Pete. “Please can we make some *now?*”

At last the day came.
"Now I think we really are ready," said Pete.
"I think you're right," Mum agreed.

The sandwiches were made.
The flapjacks smelled delicious.
The jelly wobbled well...
and the birthday cake looked *wonderful!*

Two days later a letter came for Pete.

"It takes a long time to plan a party!" Pete sighed.
"You're right," said Mum.
"But it was a great party!" added Pete.
"You're right," Mum said.